Ulrich von Mende

Design Classics

The VW Golf

KU-273-570

Verlag form

April 1971. What was rolling there was to also serve as the basis for a competent successor to the Karmann *Ghia*, the highly successful sport coupé based on the *Beetle* chassis.

What was drafted by Giugiario was determined by the package stipulation, i.e., the arrangement of the engine position, the passenger space and body type, here the hatch-back. Since the Porsche version EA 266 had already started with this prerequisite, similarities couldn't be avoided. But the character of an automobile is really determined by the details. The EA 266 stressed the front fender with round headlights and had only a slightly broken-up side view without strengthening seam. The line of the window opening was drawn with a curve, the rear was steep and the front window had an appropriately stronger angle – a closed form that in no way hinted at the *Beetle's* form. The novelties shouldn't just show beneath the metal but also in the metal.

During the development of the *Beetle's* successor, VW also had to work on the theme of corporate management, which was almost as important. Lotz, who had brought Giugiaro to Wolfsburg and didn't come from the automobile industry himself, no longer had any patrons on the supervisory board or in the public. The model palette had become too expensive because it was technically too diverse. It was the Audi-NSU boss, Rudolf Leiding, who succeeded Lotz in the fall of 1971. He cleaned up the model palette, and it was he who terminated the developmental work at Porsche. He also had another version, developed parallel to the front drive model, from which the later Audi 50 and VW Polo evolved.

Fortunately, there is a museum: the Porsche proposal as an object of antiquity.

Following page: in the beginning was the egg – a shape that can not be improved. But with corners and a 30 cm reduction in length, everything can be packed together in a better way: engine, suitcases and five passengers.

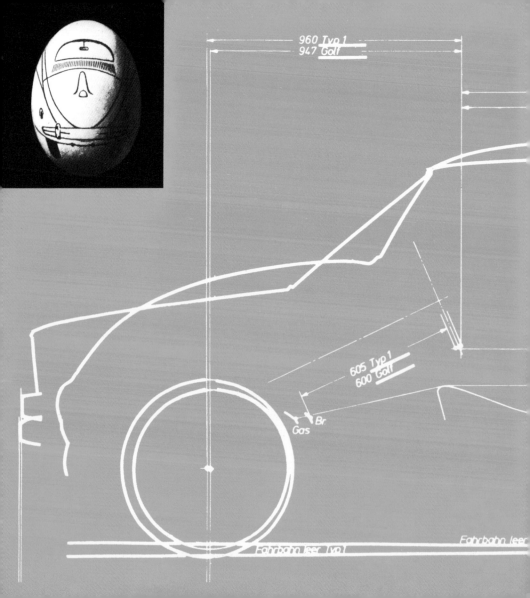

960 Typ 1
947 Golf

605 Typ 1
600 Golf

Br.
Gas

Fahrbahn leer Typ 1   Fahrbahn leer

But what kind of car did Giugiaro deliver? And what burdens did it carry? The *Beetle,* worldwide, had meanwhile become a symbol for personal mobility. It was technically undemanding, notwithstanding the fact that hardly a single component went unchanged by the time it reached the end of its life, which inexorably expanded the inventory of spare parts. Formally, though, it was always a *Beetle,* even when it received a panoramic front window treatment, or huge, circular taillights. The *Beetle* remained the classless car; but in its convertible version, it could hold its own on the island of Sylt even next to a Ferrari. What would the successor of a car that makes the claim, "there are forms that can't be improved," possibly look like? To make this claim plausible, the huge picture of an egg displaying the back of a *Beetle* was placed above the heading.

The successor that was suggested by Giugiaro could not continue the *Beetle* line in a conceptual way. In the same spirit as the 1998 New *Beetle* advertisement, "Back is now front," the design concept for the *Beetle* successor was also determined: "Round is now square." Little documentation material is left to reconstruct the genesis of the idea – literally. Some blue chalk drawings and a few photographs of the various models have been preserved. Both have in common the fact that the egg of the *Beetle* became the box of the successor. The *Beetle,* built by the millions with a 240 cm wheel base and 130 cm track, also determined the formats for the workshops and car lifts that formed the tight VW dealership network. A successor had to take this fact into account. Hence, the new

one had an identical wheelbase of 240 cm, but its track grew by 9 cm to 139 cm.

Anything in between is interesting. Whereas in the early fifties the *Beetle,* with its rounded back and 150 cm height, looked almost like a small car next to the Fords and Opels, and whereas its rounded back and front made us forget the 407 cm length, a box can not lie. Certainly, a sphere contains the largest volume within the smallest surface area, but the Beetle – a semi-sphere with running boards – couldn't optimally take advantage of this geometric quality. Okay. There was room for four adults, and there was a small trunk in the front and that storage area behind the back seat, but the package, the design of the volume to accommodate people, engine and luggage between four wheels, could definitely be improved.

A direct comparison showed that the abilities of the *Beetle's* volume to carry people and luggage had to be optimized. Its successor needs only 370 cm and 5 millimeters to successfully accomplish this between its bumpers. 7 additional centimeters in width can work miracles if they are completely given to the interior. In the case of the original *Beetle,* due to the width of the running boards, its interior was still cramped; the 154 cm width of the car didn't completely offer itself to the interior.

Amazingly – or perhaps not – the *Beetle's* successor had almost the exact same measurements as all the other models on the market that combined the technical concepts of front engine, front drive and notchback. By the end of the sixties, VW had a model, with an interior, that was ready to

Preceding page: the Golf from Italy as a 1:1 scale model.

Egg or box, both need eyes – Herbert Schäfer had recognized this, quite correctly.

A flat air-cooled boxer motor in the rear became upright, in-line and water-cooled in the nose: the Golf engine.

roll, but they didn't have drive train for it. Formally, however, it was imbalanced. A notchback, similar to a Fiat 127, and pulled down pretty far, didn't quite harmonize with the rear side windows, which became larger towards the top thus fashioning the C-column into an inverted triangle. This is a detail that was improved later by the Peugeot 205 and redis-covered in 1998 by Fiat Seicento, yet it was never optimized. Whereas the wheel openings already had the clear circular shape with strong fender lips, the window frames of the doors couldn't make up their mind between rounded and sharp edges.

This is what made the original Golf: thick C-column, edgy nose, cicular wheel openings.

Following double page: a puzzle. What distinguishes the production model from the Giugiaro-Golf?

The concept that Giugiaro presented in the summer of 1971 as a 1:1 scale model was based on construction sket-ches of the development model EA 337 with a four-cylinder engine and transmission. But the common features went no further. The concept by Ital-Design – the correct name of Giugiaro's design office – was the clear box. A strongly slanted hood, an almost elegantly slanted front window, two clearly outlined side window surfaces above a smooth, only slightly bulging flank, a notchback behind a large C-column, everything above clear, rounded wheel openings as in the in-house version – these were the characteristics that were preserved in the serial production.

What was abandoned? Herbert Schäfer, a car-body spe-cialist with a talent for automobile design who had been with VW for many years, was given the chance of a lifetime. With the development of the *Beetle's* successor, the design department was expanded to a professional size. His work, and perhaps also his greatest achievement, was to interfere

Golf and Scirocco front end – the family ties are unmistakable.

The multimillion deal: the original Golf from 1974 hits the roads of the world in such clear and edgy attire.

with Giugiaro's work so carefully that the concept was preserved but the new body became a character. What were these refinements?

They were actually simplifications. Taking into consideration the American safety standards, the roof was extended by 70 mm; hence, the angle of the windshield became a bit steeper. Giugiaro's suggestion of rectangular lights were presented by the competition almost ad nauseum, and clear circles were deemed better. At first, they were widely placed and centered in the rectangle of the grille, and the vertical glass surfaces of the turn indicators were positioned at the corners – a motif allowed for the coupé version, the *Scirocco*. For the production series, the turn indicators moved down into the bumper, and the circular lights were moved further out towards the edges, which broadened the face somewhat. The thin, chromed bumpers in Giugiaro's version still had vertical "horns" extending downward in order to intercept the different bumper heights of the competition that dared to get too close.

Where Giugiaro had restricted the two side windows with thin frames and very tight radii at the corners, the lines were more strongly drawn for the production model. The glass surfaces were divided with vertical webs but without designing the resulting glass triangles to be movable. In both the two-door and the four-door version, an angled terminating edge was added to the rear side windows' bottom corners at the C-column, similar to the motif in BMW models. This provided the back doors of the four-door version with a more favorable design.

24

Only little needed to be changed in nine years: in 1978 the noticeably more elegant bumpers were introduced, in 1980, wider taillights. Both were good enough until 1983.

Klappe auf. Klappe zu.

Wenn Sie beim Golf die Heckklappe auf-
machen, eröffnen Sie sich einen großen und
breiten Gepäckraum von 350 Litern.

Die hinteren Sitze können so geklappt und
geschwenkt werden, daß Sie in kürzester Zeit
doppelt so viel Gepäckraum haben: 700 Liter.

Und wenn Sie den Golf ausnahmsweise bis
unter das Dach vollpacken müssen, haben Sie
alles in allem gut 1.000 Liter, um auch sperri-
ges Gepäck unter Dach und Fach zu bringen.
(Vergessen Sie allerdings den zweiten Außen-
spiegel nicht.)

Weil der Golf Motor und Getriebe vorn
hat, sind auch bei vollem Gepäckraum die
Antriebsräder noch gut belastet. Und das
Heck hängt nicht durch.

Weder das Gewicht noch die Menge zwin-
gen den Golf in die Knie. Die langhubigen
Federbeine vorn und hinten ergeben lange
Federwege.

Und weil die Federung progressiv ausge-
legt ist, schluckt sie selbst bei voller Zuladung
Schlaglöcher und Bodenwellen.

Also keine Bescheidenheit beim
Wahrnehmen von Sonderange-
boten. Der Golf packt das schon.
Klappe auf. Klappe zu.

Golf, der Kompakt-VW. Auto, Motor und Spaß.

Where Giugiaro added three fanned gills in the C-column for ventilating the interior and slit the metal strips left and right of the lowered rear window for ventilation, the production model did away with the visible openings in the side and back – which only benefited the integrity of the entire form. Bumpers with thin rubber layers became bumpers with thick rubber layers and plastic end caps in order to grant a last bit of functionality to the U-shaped metal strip that was easily produced but still looked rather cheap.

Where Giugiaro kept silent in the 1:1 model – there were no door handles and the appropriate molds – the trapezoid-shaped molds with clearly outlined handles and covered openers that we know from the *Beetle* were being added. And where, in Giugiaro's design, the flanks softly bent similar to the Porsche predecessor, a clear groove was drawn into the metal that now held a thin rubber strip covered with chrome. One detail that was contained in both the *Passat* and the *Scirocco* already made the rear view look larger in Giugiaro's design: the tailgate merged with the sides so that the separating joint between tailgate and body wasn't visible from the back.

Whereas Giugiaro came up with wheel rims with many openings, restraint was practiced for the production model, although aesthetically they were no better. Steel rims with a silver metallic varnish and strongly contoured rectangular openings, with four visible bolts with a black plastic cap were inherited from the Beetle for the standard versions. This was functionally unfortunate, because the later use in the production model revealed rusted, scratched and

An advertiser's dream: inside larger than on the outside – although the trunk of the original Golf was only average.

A flatter, more elegant car on a Golf platform and with Golf technology: the Scirocco in the 1977 version.

quickly dirty rims that – reaching beyond the rim shoulder – often fought, and lost, battles with curbs.

What nobody wanted to believe, but what the wind tunnel and the detail work it prescribed had proven, was that the *Beetle's* successor only needed minimal aerodynamic corrections – for example, a softer, rounded edge between the nose and hood and a small, hardly noticeable front spoiler. The Cd-factor, the physical value of a volume's aerodynamic quality, was exemplary for this class of automobile, especially for this "box." The aerodynamics of the Porsche *928,* presented three years later with an eight-cylinder V8 and a top speed of 250 km/hr, was no better than what VW put onto the market in 1974 with a Cd-factor of 0.42.

The interior was kept unspectacularly simple. What caught the eye was the clearly arranged dashboard. Like the front of the car, defined by circle and rectangle, the dashboard was just as well organized. The round instruments were set into a matte-silver surface and, on either side, narrow surfaces, rounded at the ends, housed control lamps. As successful as this design may have been, the steering wheel and door covers were harmlessly styled. But after all: in a first attempt to judge design with objective criteria, the interior, and the dashboard especially, were awarded a prize in the 1976 design competition held by the German Design Council in connection with the "Bundespreis Gute Form."

Less rewarding was data from the automobile market, the economy, and the international situation. In the late fall of 1973 what would soon be called the oil crisis appeared on

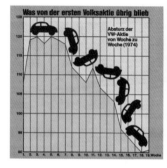

A generational leap: from the symmetrical metal dashboard of the Beetle (1950) to the instrument panel of the Golf.

The Beetle nosedives: VW stock plummeted along with the numbers of registrations. High time for the Golf.

the scene, and it was followed by driving bans and empty autobahns; overnight, the gas price increased by an outrageous 12%, which makes the 6 Pfennig increase in 1999 look like peanuts. These were the worst startup conditions imaginable for a car that was to make a name for itself as the Beetle's successor. Its technical twin, the Scirocco, had to be presented to the press in March 1974 on the company test grounds of VW in Ehra-Lessin near Wolfsburg due to impending driving bans. The economy also offered only a dismal outlook: a new bankruptcy record, 7% inflation, 1 million unemployed and an 18% production decline at VW – the Beetles successor simply had to get going. The *Golf.*

Right! *Golf* was the name of the Beetle successor. After *Passat* and *Scirocco,* it was to be yet another windy name. Blizzard had been discussed, but the ski manufacturer with the same name didn't play along. The age-old problem: find a name that not only has to fit but is also free of any preassociations. *Golf* was the solution. Everybody can understand and pronounce it, worldwide. May 1974 approached. White clouds and blue Bavarian skies – the Nymphenburg Castle in Munich was the background for the press premiere.

What followed was first concern and then hope. From the valley of sorrow where the *Beetle* desperately tried to survive, the *Golf* rapidly drove towards success, although it lost to the easily rusting *Alfasud* in early comparison tests. The *Golf* also rusted, like no VW before it. And reader's letters complained about its tight backseats, bad front seats, the trunk. Many had nothing but snide remarks to make: was this really going to be the *Beetle's* successor? But the

This child needed a name: not a windy blizzard but a solid Golf.

Technology properly packaged: engine crosswise in the front, shocks and flat rear axle steering coupling measured 30 cm less than the Beetle.

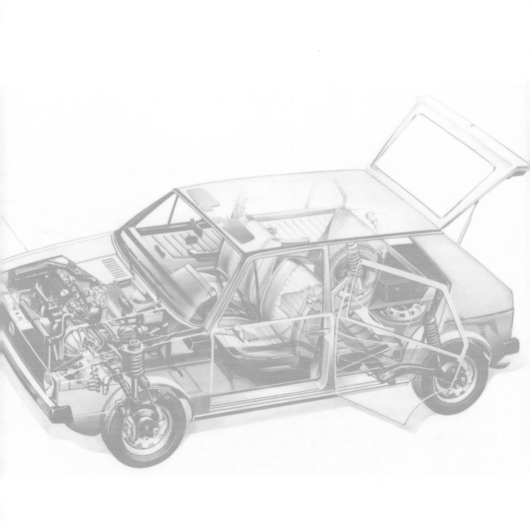

miracle happened, the *Golf* became as classless as the *Beetle* before it, and it wasn't just any successor. In 1974 Germany became world champions in soccer with a 2:1 win against Holland; and the *Golf,* too, turned onto the front straightaway, racing towards the checkered flag.

When the *Golf* was launched, 16.5 million *Beetles* had been built. In October of 1976 the milestone of one million was reached, only one month after the presentation of the legendary Golf diesel, the pacemaker for all diesel engines in the compact car class. A convertible presented in St. Tropez during the spring of 1979 rang in the third *Golf*-million in September. In February of 1982 the number had risen to five million, and in April the production of the *Caddy* began, the pick-up version of the *Golf.* Today, we're already living in the fourth generation of the *Golf* – with a notchback, as a station wagon, with four-wheel drive, four-cylinder, six-cylinder and more. 17 million cars had been built by November 1996.

And then there was the *GTI.* Two years after the market launch, a hot 110 PS version was conceived. The marketing strategists estimated that they would be able to sell only 5000 copies. It turned out to be over one million, all of them setting the new standard for fast compact cars. In the beginning it was distinguished on the outside only with a somewhat larger front spoiler, wider strips on the flanks and the unmistakable thin, red-painted frame of the front grill.

With its incredible success, the *Golf* broke with its format. After a quarter century and four series, 820 kg empty weight turned into 1163 kg, 370 cm length became 415 cm,

A success story in and of itself: the GTI. After the first tests, the press spoke respectfully of the Golf in sheep's clothing.

The Golf didn't have the potential for variety, but it made a convertible and pickup version. The station wagon had to wait until Golf three came along.

The original Golf had a tight layout; therefore, the Golf 2 had to create space without denying its predecessor.

Following double page: when designers dream... Reality will take care of it in the end – for example, the form of the wheels.

13-inch wheels became 14-inch wheels, DM 9,350 became DM 25,700. However, the *Golf* had attained classless status. Similar to the *Beetle* in its design approach, the window frames, the round wheel openings, the purely functional solutions of the front and back, have that kind of austerity that doesn't seek out prestige and therefore signal a classless standing and, in the end, make for good design.

The success of the *Golf* lives from the well-timed changes in models. The *Beetle* was continuously – but almost unnoticeably – improved in its details, but it was always the *Beetle*. Hence, it could never shake its inherent disadvantages out of the metal. Action, however, was taken in time in the case of the *Golf*. The re-edition was to and had to guarantee competitiveness and thus the future of the technical and formal concept. Each redevelopment, from *Golf 2* to *Golf 4*, asked the same questions. Does a new *Golf* have to be as radically new when compared with the preceding model as the *Golf* had to be compared with the *Beetle*? And is the idea of a gradually changing model family that is still recognizable as "*Golf*" future-oriented enough? Meanwhile, the enduring success of the fourth-generation *Golf* shows that the decision for the *Golf* concept, its continual development and re-interpretation, was the right one.

Whereas the *Golf 2* remained close to the first *Golf* in a formal sense, the design of the *Golf 3* was more courageous. Also, this was done in order for it to become even more aerodynamic. In the rear it was given a stronger termination line at the bottom, and a more rounded nose improved the aerodynamics – by abandoning the almost classical round

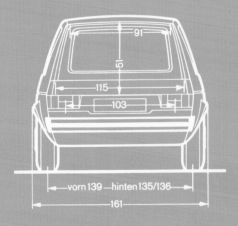

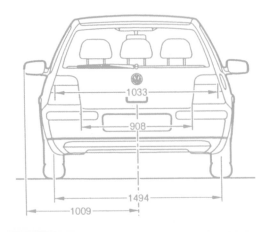

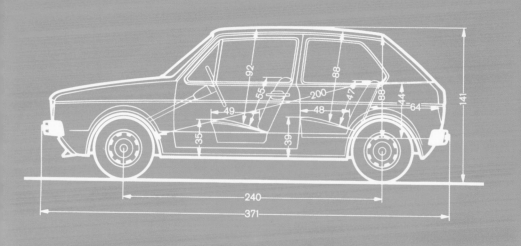

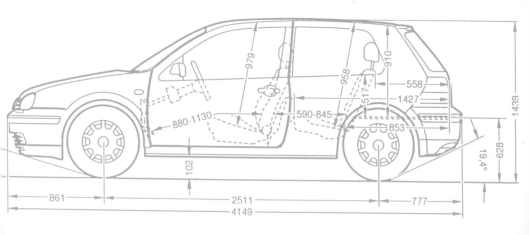

eyes. But good design can hold its own; the new headlight contour hasn't caused the *Golf* to loose face.

The *Golf 4* was the first newcomer in the *Golf* family that was no longer escorted by the chief designer Herbert Schäfer. Hartmut Warkuß, who blew the bourgeois dust off Audi's bodies, became Schäfer's successor and the father of the Golf 4. His debut was, however, the *Passat 5*, the best proposal to move VW design ahead – away from formal standards that, at least in production VWs, didn't look toward the Avant-garde.

For the *Golf 4*, Warkuß established the motto: back to the roots. This meant preserving the continuity of a car with a special position. This also meant reinterpreting the design quality of *Golf 1* in a way that its outstanding characteristics wouldn't be lost. For Warkuß, this also meant great praise for the *Golf 1*. The 4-series now appears in a clear, striking form that doesn't have to seek refuge in stretched out seams and stabilizing steps. The narrow joints of the hood and doors logically lay themselves on top of the metal skin. The glass surfaces of the lights and windows are strikingly integrated in the front and, especially, in the rear, and this is a clear indication of quality. And it has remained a true *Golf* – with a long roof, steep back and thick C-column, the face close to that of the 3-series; the family tree has grown, but it hasn't sprouted. Everybody can tell right away: here comes a *Golf*.

The *Golf* is proof that evolution doesn't leave enough room for innovation, and that well-proven elements can be reinterpreted in a contemporary formal language. And only

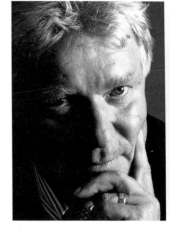

Preceding double page: the economic miracle Golf: 25 years led to a track that is 11 cm wider but a wheelbase 444 mm greater in length; Golf 1 and 4 in a scaled comparision.

The Golf 4 (since 1997) cleverly hides its tight track beneath 411 cm of body length, extremely fine seams confirm the claim: "as of a piece."

Hartmut Warkuß, head of design at VW, presents the Golf 4, thus far the most consequential interpretation of the original model.

because of this permanent renewal is the *Golf* concept, born 25 years ago, still valid today.

Photo Credits
p. 2: Giugiaro Design, s. p. a.; p. 4, 5, 8: Der Spiegel 38/1974; p. 2, 14, 28, 34, 40, 41, 44, 45, 46: VW-Archiv; p. 19, 31: auto, motor und sport, 2 / 1974; p. 32, 33: VW-Report 6, 1971; all other pictures by Ulrich von Mende.

Service
If you would like to receive our catalog,
please contact us:

Verlag form.
Books & Magazines on design issues.

Telephone +49 (0) 69 94 33 25-0
Facsimile   +49 (0) 69 94 33 25-25
e-Mail: form@form.de
http://www.form.de

Imprint:
©1999 Verlag form GmbH,
Frankfurt am Main
All rights reserved, especially those of
translation into other languages.

Translated into English by:
Katja Steiner and Bruce Almberg

Editor:
Volker Fischer

Editorial Department:
Frank Zimmer

Graphic Design:
Susanne Baumgarten,
CBCD Cool Blue Corporate Design,
Frankfurt am Main

Lithographie:
Hans Altenkirch
Mediaproduktionen GmbH,
Nieder-Olm

Print:
Graspo
Zlín, Tschechien

Die Deutsche Bibliothek –
CIP-Einheitsaufnahme
The VW Golf / Ulrich von Mende. [Transl. into
Engl. by Katja Steiner and
Bruce Almberg. Ed.: Volker Fischer]. –
Frankfurt am Main : Verl. Form, 1999
(Design Classics; 20)
Dt. Ausg. u. d. T.: Der VW-Golf
Einheitssacht.:
ISBN 3-931317-89-7